CELEBRATIONS

POEMS OF
LIFE AND LOVE

KATHRYN CAROLE ELLISON

Published by Lady Bug Books, an imprint of Brisance Books Group.
Lady Bug Press and the distinctive ladybug logo are registered trademarks of
Lady Bug Books, LLC.

Lady Bug Books
400 112th Avenue N.E.
Suite 230
Bellevue, WA 98004
www.ladybugbooks.com

For information about custom editions, special sales and permissions, please contact
Brisance Books Group at specialsales@brisancebooksgroup.com

Manufactured in the United States of America
ISBN: 978-1-944194-06-2

First Edition: May 2016

A NOTE FROM THE AUTHOR

The poems in this book were written over many, many years...
as gifts, of sorts, to my children. I began writing them in the
1970s, when my children were reaching the age of reason and
as I found myself in the position of becoming a single parent.
I needed something special to share with them—something that
would become a tradition, a ritual they could always count on...

And so the Advent Poems began—one day, decades ago—
with a poem 'gifted' to them each day during the December
holiday season every year. The poems were accompanied by a
little trinket or sweet for them to enjoy. Forty years later... my
children still look forward to the poems that started a family
tradition that new generations have come to cherish.
(Or is it the trinkets they love?)

It's my sincere hope that you will embrace and enjoy them
as we have and share them with those you love.

Children of the Light was among the first poems I wrote and
is included in each of my *Poems of Life and Love* books:
Heartstrings, Inspirations, and *Celebrations.* After writing
hundreds of poems, it is still my favorite. The words came
from my heart and my soul and flowed so effortlessly that it
was written in a single sitting. All I needed to do was capture
the words on paper. *Light,* to me, represented all that was
good and pure and right with the world, and I believed then—
as I do today—that those elements live in my children...
and perhaps in all of us. We need only to dare...

DEDICATION

To my parents: Herb and Bernice Haas

Mom, you were the poet who went before me...
unpublished, but appreciated nonetheless.

And Dad, you always believed in me,
no matter what direction my life took.
Thank you for your faith in me,
and for your unconditional love.

TABLE OF CONTENTS

LIFE'S JOYS

LIFE'S LESSONS

LIFE'S GIFTS

LIFE'S JOYS

THE HAPPINESS HABIT

Happiness is such a nebulous thing –
It comes and goes on a whim.
It's pretty much where you find it;
It depends on where you 'swim.'

Since there's nothing more invigorating
Than to share a happy space,
Be sure to put yourself with people
Who wear a happy face.

A contribution you can make
Which will add to the happiness habit
Is to make sure your words fall gently
Upon another's spirit.

Gracious words add beauty
To the environment, yes they do.
Like begets like, so say kind words.
Happiness begins with you.

And what is true, this one last thing,
Which I will now append.
Your happiness is bound to be doubled
When you share it with a friend.

RITUALS

Rituals are central to our lives
Whether we recognize them or not –
They're used when major events occur
To essentially 'mark the spot.'

They're also used in daily chores
Like the preparation of a meal.
A person might use them in business
When firming up a deal.

Rituals give us places to be playful in life;
To explore meaning in what we do;
And time to rebuild family relationships,
Time to mend and glue.

Rituals connect us with our past;
They define our lives in the present.
They show us our path to the future,
Which we can make more pleasant.

As we pass on our ceremonies and traditions
To the next generation in line,
We tie together branches of the family tree
And use our love as twine.

CHILDREN OF THE LIGHT

There are those souls who bring the light,
Who spill it out for all to share,
And with a joy that does excite
They show the world that they do care.
It is so very bright.

In this sharing, love does pervade
Into their lives and cycles 'round;
And as this light is outward played
The love is also inward bound.
It is an awesome trade.

You are a soul whose light is shared.
It comes from deep within your heart.
It's best because it is not spared,
Because it's total, not just part.
And I am glad you've dared.

Author's Note:

Of all the poems I have written to and about my children,
this one is my favorite.

The Greek Muse Erato was present the evening I put ink
to paper to write *Children of the Light* and I shall never
forget the feeling of focus and attention as the words
spilled out onto the page.

Not a word has been changed in this poem from the
night it was written. I believe that my children truly
are *Children of the Light*, and everything I am
as a mother I owe to them.

It is "an awesome trade."

– KCE

LOVE AS A VERB

Proactive people make 'love' a verb.
Love is something you do.
The sacrifice you make, the giving of self –
Love is active, it is constant and true.

Don't wait for love to come to you;
Give it without any thought
Of whether it will be returned in kind.
By you, it should never be sought.

RHYTHM

You can hear it in the street and
You can feel it on the mountain.
You can sense it when you greet and
You can taste it in the fountain.

You are making your own rhythm
Through whatever moves you make.
And it's not like any other.
There's no chance for a mistake.

Yes, your rhythms are your own
And your dances please me greatly,
Whether in a pas de deux, or
Dancing solo and stately.

Your rhythm's with you everywhere
In every step you'll ever take.
It stays with you for all your days.
It's yours alone. Make no mistake.

KINDNESS

Kind words can be short and easy to speak,
But their echoes are truly endless.
Kindness doesn't have any boundaries.
And with it you'll never be friendless.

Plato suggested, on the importance of kindness,
That people you meet might be needing a smile.
Assuming that everyone you meet is fighting a battle,
It's better to reach out, to go the extra mile.

Tenderness and kindness, not signs of weakness,
Are the embodiment of strength and resolution.
Never lose a chance to share a kind word.
It's everything to someone. Make it your contribution.

Courage. Kindness. Friendship. Character.
These qualities define us as human creatures.
On occasion they can propel us to greatness.
Keep kindness, my dears, as one of your features.

When you know yourself to be connected to all,
Acting with kindness is a natural thing to do.
Love grows only by sharing it with others.
It's never wasted when it comes through you.

Kindness is a language blind and deaf can understand.
In action it's a thrill to behold.
The most difficult thing to give away is kindness,
For it is usually returned tenfold.

RAP

Got all dressed up
On a Saturday night
Was feeling good
We were not up tight.

My dress was red
His shirt was new
It matched his eyes
They were baby blue.

The band was great
The music sweet
We danced and danced
We were on our feet.

He held me tight
All evening long.
Everything was right
I could do no wrong.

And then...
And then...
And then...
And then...

Out of the blue
Without any warning
The alarm went off
And it was morning.

I couldn't remember
How the evening ended.
The dream was over
My life depended
On getting back to sleep
And dreaming on...

Was his name Steve
Or was it John
I don't remember
His name, but then
Maybe I'll dream
About it all again.

TRUE FRIENDS

About true friends: there are lots of them –
Some you do not know today.
As you go along your life's path in joy,
They'll show up, share a smile, and stay.

They'll enrich your lives as you do theirs,
'Cause you'll love them and let them go
To pursue their goals and find their path;
And they'll always be part of your 'show.'

True friends leave a legacy, a part of them
Is left behind in your heart.
And when reunion occurs and paths cross again
It's as if you were never apart.

True friendship knows no time restrictions,
Nor space; there's no feeling of 'other.'
True friends express unconditional love.
Oh, children, I'm glad I'm your mother.

To watch you grow and make your ways
Expanding into your universe of perfection.
Your friends are extensions of who you are.
They're an amazing spiritual collection.

PLAY, PLAY, PLAY

When you were a child, life was oh, so sweet.
Each morning you'd wake and land on your feet.
With joy in each step and a heart so pure
You'd set out for that day's amazing adventure.

You didn't think of what needed to be done.
You simply did things, one by one.
Oh, that you could continue today...
The joy, the habits... the ability to play!!

Of course you can, it's in your nature
To live in the world as a playful creature.
The stresses of life are dimmed and repressed
If you can see life's humor and live with zest.

Get back in touch with your playful selves.
Put your burdens behind you – up on the shelves!
Playing makes everything so very sweet.
Each morning you'll wake happy and land on your feet!

SUCCESS

What is success?
Can you define it?
Can you taste it?
Or can you touch it?

Does it elude you?
Does it embrace you?
Do you seek it?
Are you afraid?

Does it depend
On something else?
Is it relative to
What others say?

No, no, you say!
Success is a feeling
Of being of value...
Of happiness in what you do.

CIRCLES

I threw a rock into a lake;
It made a wondrous sound.
And from the center ripples moved;
The designs were O-shaped – round.

This image mirrors a community
In its patterns of evolving.
Concentric circles on the move –
Forever in motion, revolving.

Influence moves in much the same way
As the rock thrown into the lake.
The movement starts from the center.
Of that, make no mistake.

Family first, and then our school,
Followed by the town and the state –
Then expanding to country and continent,
Until it's the world we consecrate.

When our community includes the whole world,
We create harmony and understanding.
We can be more accepting and less judgmental,
Giving peace more room for expanding.

BE THE CHANGE

We are given a job to do in life
When we are born, when we enter this place.
We're all assigned a piece of the garden
To grow and maintain, and embrace.

In growing this garden we're meant to transform –
To improve it from how it was found.
And do our best with what tools we are given
To make changes quite simple – or profound.

Our garden is our very own life –
Our relationships, our work, our abode,
And our current circumstances – as they are –
To be tended and watered and hoed.

Every situation we find ourselves in
Is an opportunity to teach
That love is better than fear – any day –
And then practice what we preach.

LIFE'S LESSONS

HONESTY

Genuine people don't have to worry
That something might slip out.
Secrets are seldom productive;
It's not what friendship is about.

Speak truth with friends and don't be afraid;
With confidence you will meet.
If you tiptoe around the heart of the matter
You'll end up with very sore feet.

Stating your case in a firm honest manner,
Without accusation or fear
Keeps the dialogue going, and opens hearts;
Then your differences will disappear.

MIRRORING

The qualities you admire most in a friend
Are worth your while to review.
While they appear to be all about him or her,
They speak volumes, my dear, about you.

The same goes when you are getting an ˙earful˙
From someone about your good friend.
They're not telling you much about your pal –
It's about them and their ability to offend.

Ever wondered how much you are giving to
The relationships you share with friends?
You can bet you are giving about the same
As what you get back in dividends.

RELATIONSHIPS

Much has been said about relationships;
They don't blossom and deepen without work.
Both parties have an obligation
That neither one can shirk.

Being cute and clever with the words you share
Can be ever so much fun,
But make sure you are on the construction crew
– And not the demolition one.

Whenever you have a complaint to make,
Try turning it into a compliment, instead.
It keeps the conversation open.
In the long run, you both come out ahead.

When a difference of opinion occurs in life
Between two friends who are headstrong,
Among the most powerful of words are these:
"I'm sorry. I was wrong."

People don't change unless they want to.
You know that, don't you? Of course,
If you feel the need to change a zebra's stripes,
Maybe you should have bought a horse!

FORGIVENESS

"Don't drag yesterday's clutter into today,"
Is advice so sound and true.
To bring yesterday's stuff to the here and now
Can only make everyone blue.

It's said that those who deserve our forgiveness
The least are the ones who need it the most.
If that's true, then to get into today free and clear,
Just forgive and go on, and don't boast.

There is nothing so freeing as to live and let live;
Forgive others their weaknesses and faults.
Just be sure to heed the lessons you've learned –
Save the knowledge in your treasure vaults.

The most loving thing you can do for another
Is to forgive him or her for a wrong deed.
Remember, the smartest people you meet
Are in school for life... so proceed.

HAVING BY DOING

No one ever attained inner harmony
By pondering the experience of others.
Wisdom does not come to us
By reading about another's.

No, it's the mistakes, the dead-end moves,
That are the portals of discovery;
An opportunity to learn, my dears,
A chance for recovery.

Wisdom does not come to us
Until we pass through the fire.
The journey is one we must take on our own
And wisdom we'll acquire.

If you don't enter the lion's den
You will never capture the beast.
Take great big bites – don't be afraid.
And... welcome to the feast.

STANDING TALL

Keep your head up, and walk with grace.
As a child of God, you are equal to all.
You have the right to be proud of yourself.
You're one of a kind, so stand up straight and tall.

There's lots of confusion behind the meaning
Of humility, and its interpretation.
The common, but wrong, translation of the word
Is self-disapproval or self-deprecation.

But the truth of it is, it's okay to believe
In yourself and, likewise, your own self worth.
Humility, in fact, is simply self-honesty.
It's yours to own, and it's yours from birth!!

COURTESY

No matter how well you think you know
Your nearest and dearest of all,
Courtesy in manner and speech is required –
Or you'll encounter a dangerous pitfall.

You won their heart with kind words and deeds;
You showed your very best side.
That set the pattern right there and then,
When caring and courtesy were applied.

Courtesy is the oil that keeps the wheels
Of love and friendship turning.
It keeps love fresh, it makes life good.
Courtesy keeps your heart's flame burning.

ALL THE ANSWERS

Phony expertise is neurotic;
There's only one known cure.
As soon as it's spotted
Make sure it's boycotted.
Ignore it. It won't endure.

No one has all the answers.
Pretending you do gives you grief.
It's most immodest,
And grossly dishonest.
Saying, 'I don't know' is a relief.

ATTITUDE

We receive from every experience in proportion to what we give.
The richness of our lives depends directly on perspective.
The depth of our commitment is a measure of our spoils.
The less, or more, that we'll commit is measured by our toils.

The attitude we carry into any situation
Will regulate our rate of growth in work or recreation.
But attitudes do more than that; they can make us frown or sing.
The quality of our lives depends on how we see a thing.

We make the world we find at hand... at home, at work, at play.
Our happiness depends on us and how we think each day.
Your happiness does not rely on what other people do.
Oh no, my loves, it boils down to only your point of view.

PERSONAL MERIT

Grow up! Who cares...
What others think of you?
There's no strength in depending
On others' points of view.

You have been given your own work to do.
Get to it now – don't be bothered by who's watching you.

Never depend on the admiration of others
Whether brothers or sisters, fathers or mothers.

What others think of you is not your concern.
Personal merit is not derived from what others discern.

What is really yours, and yours alone?
It's the use you make of what you own.

Your ideas, resources, and opportunities;
Your books, your tools... pursue with impunity.

Make the most of what's at hand, my friend.
Be happy with yourself and your joy will know no end.

HERE AND NOW

The past is past, kiss it goodbye;
The here is now, not tomorrow.
So live in your present indebtedness,
And you'll avoid a life of sorrow.

Do not have regrets for the past;
You know it cannot be undone.
Since tomorrow is only a contemplation,
You must live today. Make it fun.

THE SPIRIT WITHIN

The easiest thing in the world, it seems,
Is sometimes the hardest to do.
Seeking peace within, or enlightenment,
We think, requires a teacher or two.

But there is a teacher within your own being,
Enlightening you spontaneously as you go.
It is there to guide you through each day,
And advises you in ways you may never know.

Remember that what you are looking for
Is what's actually doing the looking.
It's not what the eye sees, but what *makes* it see.
It is the Spirit ... (Ah... now you're 'cooking!')

HELP YOURSELF

If you set out to make a big mark
To set the world on fire;
To be the savior of all the world,
For all to adore and admire.
You'll fail – you will – not from lack of trying
But from the motive in your desire.

Truly helping others results
When you have made your own way.
Your personal success is yours alone,
And it fills your resume.
You're on your own to get where you're going;
You alone must 'pay to play.'

By doing your own work you find your way
That others might emulate.
By pursuing your path, and yours alone,
You find your realized state.
Your path is there in front of you
For you to navigate.

BLIND FAITH

When things go wrong I sometimes feel
That God is giving me a bad deal;
I wonder what indeed is real.

It's said, however, when things go 'bad,'
And we get worked up and very sad
That faith in the outcome can be 'had.'

A smiling face, a hopeful air
Will lighten a load that's hard to bear,
And open a way; if we but dare

To place our trust in One so wise.
Our chances for success will rise
And lead us onward to new highs.

A little blind faith will take us far.
It will boost our lives beyond just par,
Bringing within reach our every star.

LIFE'S GIFTS

THE GIFT OF LIFE

Each day we will be called to give
A gift of ourselves that measures worth;
So that each moment that we live
We'll learn the truths as we go forth.

The gift of life is an obligation
To give the best we have inside;
Our efforts, talents – all a donation
To whatever glides along the tide.

From giving our best we are to gain
The lessons we must learn to grow.
There'll be some joy; there'll be some pain;
But in the end, the truth we'll know.

There's no guarantee we'll enjoy the ordeal,
But here's something to allay our fears:
When we are ready, the truth will reveal;
"When the student is ready, the teacher appears."

LIFE FOOD

If everything you encounter is your life,
You must ask yourself this question:
"What kinds of 'life food' will I eat today?
Is it good for my digestion?"

Ask yourself what kind of ideas are you
Taking into your marrow and bone.
Are they healthy and wholesome or ones for which
You may some day need to atone?

Life's not a matter of having less,
And going without your needs;
Nor about having more to embellish your lives
As you, through your life, proceed.

It's about paying attention to the elements
That make up your lives each day;
And asking how you can respond to your world
With respect along the way.

YOUR LIFE STORY

Suppose a movie was made of your life,
And all the relationships you have had.
And when it was shown on the big wide screen,
Would you be happy or sad?

We seem to choose people to be in our lives
So that we can learn and grow.
Sometimes it doesn't turn out as we'd hoped,
But at least we gave it a go.

For me, I know that there have been
Many, many mistakes on my part.
I am in hope the errors were innocent,
And I escaped with a pure heart.

I read this thought once, and it seems to be true:
"If measuring your relationship is a concern –
You can tell how much you are giving to it
By how much you get in return."

It's good to be a friend, and to be trusted to grow –
And learn and change along the way.
How will your friends who are closest to you
Write your obituary some day?

GIVING AND RECEIVING

The concept of exchanging energy
Is simply that you reap what you disperse.
Relationships where trading is not free
Are not those in which you'd want to be.
Resentments only make the matters worse;
So, keeping things in balance is the key.

The ideal is to barter without scheme;
To give without a thought of what's in store.
In turn, you're blessed with more than you can dream.
It's in proportion to your living theme.
You're blessed in correlation, less or more,
In meaningful relations, it would seem.

LIGHT

Let the beauty of your soul travel the earth
To provide light for others in the dark.
Show others how to live by being an example –
As you live your life, lend a spark.

Choose joy, choose happiness – a zest for life!
Love others; make your own Shangri-La.
Light your lamp. It's bright! A beacon of hope,
Till they can find their own formula.

Your light will change your own path as well,
And hasten you on toward perfection.
By helping others along the way
Everyone grows from the connection.

RENEWED ENERGY

Sometimes when I am feeling slow
And think that I am tired,
I find that I'm not in the flow.
Into myself I'm mired.
Preoccupation is single,
And I don't mingle.
Energy flags.
Spirit drags.

If I can get outside of me
My spirit is restored.
If I can at long last get free
I am no longer bored.
If I had my druthers,
I'd surely think of others.
Energy pours!
Spirit restores!

EXERCISE YOUR IMAGINATION

A fresh perspective is needed to lead you
Around a stumbling block in your path
When logic and reason, based on what you know,
Bring negative results in the aftermath.

Beyond logic there exists your imaginative skills
To join symbols together in a new way.
They throw new light on the problem at hand,
And bring resolution without much delay.

Your imagination is a discovering ability
To see relationships in a totally new light;
To see new meanings which are special and true
And to apply them when the time is right.

ABILITY TO LOVE

Another thing to add to the list of
Qualities with which you are blessed:
Your ability to love and be loved in return –
Something you've always possessed.

To be able to dwell with love in your heart
And to share it without measure
Is one of the greatest skills there is.
It creates a circle of pleasure.

I've said it before, and I'll say it again:
You both teach me so much – it's true –
About unconditional love and its rewards.
(I look at life and see a more loving view.)

We need all the love that this world has to offer.
It makes us grow up straight and strong.
It helps us to understand, as I'm sure you know,
The difference between right and wrong.

BE STILL, BE DIVINE

We are most awake when our minds are still,
When we've let go of the past;
When future and past no longer matter
And the present is here at last.

Reserve ten minutes twice a day
To quiet your mind and seek peace;
To stop all voices that nag at your soul;
To bring quiet so that all noises cease.

It's a still mind that's an awakened mind,
And an alert mind, full of boundless love.
It's a Divine Mind, according to some,
Filled with love from heaven above.

JUST AS YOU ARE

We become what we think about...
... all day long.
We believe what we tell ourselves...
... all day long
Our lives take on aspects of what we say...
... all day long.

So fill your hearts with thoughts of love...
... and then become them.
So tell yourself only words of love...
... and then become them.
Accept yourself for the miracles you are...
... and then become them.

To yourself, say, "I love you with all of my heart...
... just as you are."
To yourself, say, "You're perfect in every way...
... just as you are."
To yourself, say, "You're deserving of love today...
... just as you are."

IMAGES AND IMAGINATION

Inside each and every one of us
Are stories waiting to be told.
They're filled with vivid images,
Their wonders to behold!

You're a storyteller by your birthright,
Like every human being.
You've an unending supply of story themes,
And you can talk about anything!

It's important for you to draw upon
The images you've acquired,
Then tell your stories to those you meet.
Nothing more is required.

Now close your eyes and see yourself
Telling a story out loud.
What is it about? And who is there?
I'll bet you've drawn a crowd.

ANGELS

It seems the belief in angels is
An 'either yes or no' opinion.
Though they've been written about for centuries
They remain in the spiritual dominion.

They seem to transcend every religion,
Every philosophy, every creed.
For every religion that has ever existed
Angels' existence is purported to precede.

So now, to believe or not to believe...
The decision's entirely up to you.
If you don't believe, it's quite all right.
To your beliefs you must remain true.

But, angels are not to be taken lightly,
Nor should your belief in them be.
Don't try to tame them into something so bland
That you cannot let them be free.

COMMUNICATE WITH LOVE

At last... the subject is communication;
Something we try to do every day.
We send out our words to others
With the hope they're understood in the same way.

To slice through the confusion of words
That often causes aggravation,
Send mental tendrils, or energy, too,
Along with your verbal communication.

Mental energy can convey ideas
Before they need to be expressed.
Try it with conscious deliberation;
I'm sure you'll be impressed.

And listen for thoughts and vibrations
Behind the other person's response.
So much of communication is silent
When one is expressing his wants.

Add this thought to the subject at hand;
Please make it your primary goal.
Give more thought to communion with another
And communicate with their soul.

ACTION

Art is expression, it is mind in action.
Work emerges from thought made real.
Michelangelo created the statue of David
By thinking, then acting, with zeal,

All of the world's great religions and beliefs –
The formulas, projects and dreams –
Are inert until action infuses its power.
Reality is in the doing, it seems.

The work to be done, the goals you seek,
Will be achieved by making a start.
Your ideas and ideals, expressed in action
Bring into balance your mind and your heart.

Action sculpts your life as it shapes the world.
(Michelangelo's works are on view.)
Your lives and your world are waiting for movement,
And, darlings, it begins with you.

AN UNFORGETTABLE EXPERIENCE

The 21st century is underway
And it seems to be spinning quite fast.
Don't forget to take time to live, really live,
And enjoy this world so vast.

Try not rushing around, and sit quietly
On the grass, or wherever you choose;
Switch off the mind, come back to earth;
Really look at things... and then muse.

Let your eyes see a willow, a lilac, or a cloud.
See how buds burst forth from the tree.
Keep it basic and simple as you look around,
And you will see, my loves, really see.

Through light and joy, the world opens up
And reveals its secrets to you.
It is ineffable beauty, unending creation;
An unforgettable experience, too.

COMING HOME

"Put another brick in the wall.
Build the barrier very tall.
My ego says I'm very small,
If I climbed up I'd surely fall.
My luck is bad – and that is all."

"There's no escape, I'm really stuck.
My fears have really run amok.
It's just my thing – I have no luck.
I must stay here in all the muck."

But wait, these are my ego voices.
I really do have other choices.
To know this fact, my heart rejoices.

Us to ourselves we introduce,
And welcome us home in just a truce

of Love.

A CLOSING THOUGHT

POETRY

It's the revelation
Of a sensation
That the poet
(Wouldn't you know it)
Believes to be
Felt only interiorly
And personal to
The writer who
... writes it.

It's the interpretation
Of a sensation
That was fueled by
A poet's sigh
And believed to be
Shared mutually
And personal to
The lucky one who
... reads it.

About the Author

Kathryn Carole Ellison is a former newspaper columnist
and journalist and, of course, a poet.

She lives near her children and stepchildren and their families in the
Pacific Northwest, and spends winters in the sunshine of Arizona.

You might find her on the golf course with friends, river rafting,
writing poems... or at the opera.

Late Bloomer

Our culture honors youth with all
It's unbridled effervescence.
We older ones sit back and nod
As if in acquiescence.

And when our confidence really gels
In early convalescence...
'We can't be getting old!' we cry,
'We're still struggling with adolescence!'

Acknowledgments

I have many people to thank...

First of all, my children Jon and Nicole LaFollette, for inspiring the writing of these poems in the first place. And for encouraging me to continue my writing, even though their wisdom and compassion surpass mine.

My wonderful stepchildren, Debbie and John Bacon, Jeff and Sandy Ellison, and Tom and Sue Ellison, who, with their children and grandchildren, continue to be a major part of my life and are loved deeply by me. These poems are for you, too.

Eva LaFollette, the dearest daughter-in-law one could ever wish for... and one of my dearest friends. Your encouragement and interest are so appreciated.

My good friends who have received a poem or two of mine in their Christmas cards these many years, for complimenting me on the messages in my poems. Your encouragement kept me writing.

To Kim Kiyosaki who introduced me to the right person to get the publishing process underway... that person being Mona Gambetta with Brisance Books Group who has the experience and know-how to make these books happen.

And finally, to John Laughlin, a fellow traveler in life, who encourages me every day in the writing and publishing process. John, I love having you in my cheering section!

OTHER BOOKS
by Kathryn Carole Ellison

HEARTSTRINGS

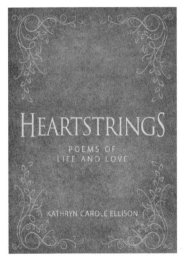

INSPIRATIONS

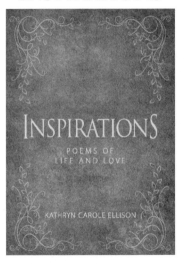